REAL LIVES

Victoria Beckham

Julia Holt

Published in association with The Basic Skills Agency

Hodder & Stoughton

A MEMBER OF THE HODDER HEADLINE GROUP

Acknowledgements
Cover: David Fisher/London Features International

Photos: pp 2 Craig Barritt/Retna; p 8 Nick Tansley/All Action; p 10 Dave Woolford/Retna; p 4 Paul Treadway/Retna; p 6 Bettmann/Corbis; p 21, 24 Reuters NewMedia Inc./Corbis; p 27 PA Photos/David Jones

Every effort has been made to trace copyright holders of material reproduced in this book. Any rights not acknowledged will be acknowledged in subsequent printings if notice is given to the publisher.

Orders; please contact Bookpoint Ltd, 130 Milton Park, Abingdon, Oxon OX14 4SB. Telephone (44) 01235 827720, Fax: (44) 01235 400454. Lines are open from 9.00–6.00, Monday to Saturday, with a 24 hour message answering service. You can also order through our website: www.hodderheadline.co.uk

British Library Cataloguing in Publication Data
A catalogue record for this title is available from the British Library

ISBN 0 340 87593 3

First published 2001
This edition published 2003
Impression number   10 9 8 7 6 5 4 3 2
Year   2007 2006 2005 2004

Typeset by SX Composing DTP, Rayleigh, Essex
Printed in Great Britain for Hodder & Stoughton Educational, a division of Hodder Headline, 338 Euston Road, London NW1 3BH by CPI Bath.

Contents

1 Introduction

Thousands of babies were born
on 4 March 1999.
But only one was called
Brooklyn Beckham.
Only one had parents
called Posh and Becks.
For that day
he was the most famous baby in the world.

Brooklyn's mum
was one of the famous Spice Girls.
She was Posh Spice.
But today everyone also knows her
by her real name.
She is Victoria Beckham.

Victoria was part of one of the biggest girl bands in the world.

2 Early Years

Victoria must be as famous
as she could ever want to be.
But she's had to work hard for it.

She was born on 17 April 1974.
She was the Adams' first child.
Their other two children
were called Louise and Christian.

Victoria started dancing classes
at the age of three.
She was happy when she was dancing.
At school she was bullied.
She felt lonely.
So at home she shut her bedroom door
and danced.

The family lived in a small village
in Hertfordshire.
The three Adams children were very close.
They played in their big swimming pool.
They had their friends round.
The two girls both wanted
to be rich and famous.
But Victoria was the one
who stuck with it.

At 16 years old she left home
to study dancing for three years at college.
She went for auditions
but she was never picked.
She was told
'You'll never make it',
or 'You're too fat'.
These days the newspapers
often say that she is too thin.

While she was at college
she fell in love
with her first boyfriend.
His name was Mark.

When Victoria was 19 years old
Mark proposed
and she said 'Yes'.

She also landed her first job
singing in a band.
They were terrible.
But it was her first break.
She still wanted to be famous
so she kept going to auditions.

3 The Spice Girls

In May 1994
Victoria was down to the last 12 girls
at an audition for an all-girl band.
She was chosen.
So she swapped one band
for another.
This time it really was her big break.

Victoria was now a Spice Girl.
She was called Posh Spice.
She was the sensible one
who kept the others' feet on the ground.
She lived with the other girls for a while
but soon moved back home.

The singing and dancing
were easy for Victoria.
She had been dancing all her life.
But the lack of free time was difficult.
In May 1995
she broke off her engagement to Mark.
She blamed her work.

The girls spent the next year
getting their songs together.
It was hard work.
But it was well worth it.
Their first single went to No. 1 in July 1996.
It went to No. 1
in 31 other countries.

The Spice Girls went straight to No. 1 with their first single.

4 Meeting David

For the rest of 1996
life was hectic for the Spice Girls.
They sang in 37 countries.

There was little time for resting.
But on 15 March 1997
Victoria was out with Mel C and sister Louise.
They were at a Manchester United match.
Manchester United had just won.
David Beckham came up to her
and said 'Hi', then he walked away.

Victoria saw that he was shy.
So she went after him.
David had seen one of her videos.
She had seen him in a magazine.
They fell in love.

Victoria met David Beckham after a Manchester United Match.

The Spice Girls
went on tour to the USA
in late 1997.

Victoria and David
were apart for a long time.
So Victoria took his No. 7 shirt
and she wore it when she rang him.
They talked on the phone
many times a day.

Soon they were making plans
for their life together.

After 10 months
they got engaged.
David said,
'As soon as I met Victoria
I knew I'd marry her.'

He looked everywhere
for the perfect ring.
He didn't find one, so he had one made.
It was a diamond-shaped diamond.

On 25 January 1998
he asked her to marry him.
She said 'Yes'.
Then she gave him a ring
and said,
'Don't forget Girl Power.
Will you marry me?'

David's team mates teased him.
They sang 'Here Comes The Bride'
when they saw him.
But he didn't care, he was happy.

Victoria and David made plans.
They bought a £300,000 flat in Cheshire.
This was near to Manchester United
so that David was close to work.
They also bought
a £2.5 million house in Hertfordshire.
This was for them to live in later,
when they had a family.

Then Victoria found out
that she was pregnant.

Victoria and David are very happy together.

5 Baby Brooklyn

Their blue-eyed baby boy was born
on 4 March 1999.
They called him Brooklyn
because Victoria found out she was pregnant
when she was in New York.

His birth was on the TV news.
Victoria and David were very happy.
Their friends sent gifts.
Elton John sent a set of silver bowls.
Mel B brought balloons
and the rest of the girls sent baby clothes.

David had a tattoo of Brooklyn's name
done on his own back.
He had Brooklyn's name
put onto his football boots
and his car seats too.

Brooklyn Bridge, New York. Victoria found out she was
pregnant in Brooklyn.

6 Wedding of the Year

As soon as they were engaged
everyone wanted to know
all about the wedding plans.
But Victoria and David
kept everything a big secret.
Even the guests
didn't know where to go
until the last minute.

They were married –
on 4 July 1999
in a castle in Dublin.
It was like a royal wedding.

The castle was lit up
with thousands of fairy lights.
There were flowers everywhere.

Victoria's beautiful cream dress
cost £60,000.
It was handmade in New York.
She wore a diamond crown.
David wore a cream suit.
They sat on thrones
in front of 236 guests
and 550 staff.

They were both very nervous
but everything went well.
They all sat down
to a lovely meal
ending with David's favourite –
sticky toffee pudding.

After the wedding
Victoria, David and Brooklyn
changed into matching purple outfits.
They had a big party.

Brooklyn was sick
on David's suit
but it didn't matter.
Everyone danced to Spice Girls hits.

It was a fairy-tale day
and it ended
with a fireworks display.

7 The Kidnap Plot

Christmas of 1999
was difficult.
Victoria and David were told
that Brooklyn was the target
of a kidnap plot.

So they found two bodyguards
to watch him.
The bodyguards live with the family.
They travel everywhere with them.

Brooklyn didn't know anything
about the kidnap plot.
He was happy playing
with his new drum kit
and his toy Ferrari.

Victoria and Brooklyn.

Early in 2000
Victoria gave Louise and Christian
a house to live in.
It's a new four-bedroomed house
in Hertfordshire
next to their parents' house.

Then David said
he had a surprise for Victoria.
It was a holiday in Italy.
They stayed with friends.
They ate pasta and watched videos.
They spent lots of time together.
It was a lovely surprise.
The holiday helped Victoria
to forget about the kidnap plot.

8 Victoria the Supermodel

Victoria was next in the news,
not for singing,
but for modelling.

Her mum and dad
and 500 other people
watched her walk down the catwalk.
She was modelling
her friend Moria's clothes.

She wore green hotpants
and then a long pink dress.
She was very nervous
but very happy.
She said she would do it again
if she was asked.
She proved to everyone
that she wasn't too fat or too thin
to be a model.

Victoria modeling for her friend and designer Moria Grachvogel.

At Brooklyn's first birthday
there were clowns and jugglers.
There were 100 guests.
It cost £12,000.

In the same month
at the Brit Awards
Victoria and the Spice Girls
were given a special award.
Then they sang some of their hits.
They were given the award
for all the work they have done
for the British music industry.

9 A Star is Born

It was an exciting year
for Victoria in 2002.
She had her second top ten hit
with 'A Mind of Its Own'.

She wrote a book about her life
called *Learning to Fly*.
It sold over 600,000 copies
and was a top ten book
for four months.

There was soon to be a new edition to this happy family.

In 1999,
Victoria had three stars
tattooed on her back.
One was for Brooklyn,
one for David,
and one for herself.

In September 2002,
she had another star done.
This was for her new son.
Victoria and David called him Romeo.

Just weeks after he was born,
the police stopped another kidnap plan.
Some men were planning to kidnap
Victoria and her boys.

Even after all this,
Victoria says she has the world at her feet.
She is rich and famous
and she has a wonderful family.
As she says,
'I'm the luckiest person alive.'